T0095596

I'm Talking to You

About Thought-Provoking Events and Places

R. NATHANIEL DUNTON

iUniverse LLC
Bloomington

I'm Talking to You
About Thought-Provoking Events and Places

iUniverse books may be ordered through booksellers or by contacting:

iUniverse
1663 Liberty Drive
Bloomington, IN 47403
www.iuniverse.com
1-800-Authors (1-800-288-4677)

Because of the dynamic nature of the Internet, any web addresses or links contained in this book may have changed since publication and may no longer be valid. The views expressed in this work are solely those of the author and do not necessarily reflect the views of the publisher, and the publisher hereby disclaims any responsibility for them.

Any people depicted in stock imagery provided by Thinkstock are models, and such images are being used for illustrative purposes only.
Certain stock imagery © Thinkstock.

ISBN: 978-1-4917-0911-5 (sc)
ISBN: 978-1-4917-0912-2 (hc)
ISBN: 978-1-4917-0913-9 (e)

Library of Congress Control Number: 2013917339

Printed in the United States of America.

iUniverse rev. date: 10/25/2013

Table of Contents

To my beloved parents, the late Mr. Robert Dunton
Sr. and the late Mrs. Mildred Mills Dunton

To my beloved wife, the late Mrs. Evelyn
Joyce Thornton Dunton

Foreword

A local Baltimore family grew up in the city just after the Great Depression of the 1930s. Much like other families, its members have gladly welcomed the present technology/social networking boom of cell phones, home computers, and other wireless communication devices. In the past, this typical American family routinely communicated one-on-one and face-to-face, as most families did during the early twentieth century.

Prior to the great electronics and technology boom, families generally sat down for their meals together, held meaningful in-person conversations, and shared and confided in one another in a substantive manner. They regularly attended church together and bonded while participating in other vigorous and fulfilled activities. During those early years, individuals would express personal affinity. That personal touch is absent from the social network (high-tech) communications world they live in today. Gone are the days of the family dinner and routine personal interaction.

Life experiences and documented historical events inspired this anthology of poems, essays, and stories. The goal is to entertain and inform you, the reader, in a sincere, truthful, and artful manner. Enjoy these works as they were developed for your personal consumption.

Anthem (Song of Life)

Sing a song to right a wrong.
Right a wrong to sing a song.
Right or wrong, sing a song.
Write along, and sing a song.
Sing that song, and right that wrong.
Sing along to write that wrong.
Write along while singing a song.
Right or wrong, you sing your song!

CHAPTER ONE

Nature

By the Lake (Reflections of a Man-Made Lake)

Someone once spoke of a country-styled oasis located in the midst of a city. It is a beautiful multipurpose man-made waterway called Lake Vantage. This lake is brilliantly located on private property within a Certified Wildlife Habitat. Spruce and weeping willow trees seemingly reach for clear skies while nestled along the lake's thriving grassy banks.

Nature proudly flaunts its beauty with a variety of plant life and floral bushings that include flowering annuals and perennial growth, representing the many colors of the rainbow.

Vertical water fountains constantly spray mists skimming the lake surface, equidistant from the water's edge, complementing this botanical setting. The pressurized water cascades into the air, creating an illusionary sky bound endless rainbow as each drop falls back into the lake, causing tiny circle of retreating ripples.

Balloon markers are strategically placed in the lake and become course markers for model boat racing. Each marker is clearly visible from a special vantage point on an observation deck and boat landing, nestled under a few shade trees just south of the lake. Lake Vantage is known for its peace and tranquility. As well, it is known for its resident families of ducks and Canadian geese. One may even get a glimpse of an oriole, that orange breast state bird, on a warm spring day. On most days, the beautiful multicolored feathered longneck geese can be observed in and around Lake Vantage. They are peacefully at home there and pay little attention to visiting observers except when being fed.

The water along the banks of Lake Vantage is rather shallow. However, the lake is stocked with catfish and a few other bottom feeders, a welcomed enhancement to the natural habitat. An occasional glimpse of a surfacing catfish is occasionally possible. No fishing is allowed.

Walkers and joggers enjoy strolling along the U-shaped, park-like trail surrounding Lake Vantage. Visitors can also relax on one of the benches conveniently facing the water.

On weekend mornings, spectators can position themselves near the lake to observe hobbyists and others participate in fun-filled model yacht boat racing. Each radio-controlled model yacht can be skillfully maneuvered through the predetermined obstacle courses. Hobbyists also occasionally use the site for flying midsized radio-controlled model airplanes. Unexpected wind, rain, and slight changes in water currents will occasionally challenge participants' skills. Whose boat will finish first? Gentlemen! Ready! Set your sails! Go!

During year-ending holidays, the lake shows yet another side of its charm. Its holiday décor is seasonally traditional, and its beauty is second to none.

Visit Lake Vantage for a special life experience where nature is a winner, but you can share this very uniquely qualified adventure.

Your Spring

Anniversaries come just once a year.
Friends and family stay.
You came into the midst of spring.
Nature seemed much livelier then.

In full bloom while birds do sing,
You're like the welcomed warmth of day
Captured in your special way,
Unending blossoms of your bliss.

Faith inspires the way you live
Through morning, noon, and night,
Proudly flaunting the fabric of your very being.

New Leaves

Through that carefree flight,
Down! Down! To the ground.
Floating, turning, and twisting in the wind,
Gliding through the swirling air,
Softly landing like feathers at journey's end.

Multicolored and more than just a few
Other mixtures cloaked from hue to hue,
Each embracing its own identity.

Draped in clusters gliding in slow-mo,
Others gently falling solo.
Trees stripped bark-less by ferocious wind and
The rain and breezes too.

In time, green leaves will bloom anew.
Trees! Trees! Trees! Barren and bare,
Smooth, crumpled, and colored leaves
Falling everywhere.

For Seasons

Look up!
See sky.
Look down!
See ground.

Dark shadows roll from skies of gray
On this vigorously balmy January day.
Cold winds and rain tap rhythmic beats,
Soaking rooftops of cars and streets.
Eyes look up again to feel
That liquid sunshine seeping in,
Tempered no less by swirling wind.

Water streams down your face,
Like ten thousand tears off to a race,
Rushing to some far-off place.
In near an instant, there's no wind nor breeze.
Warmth starts seeping through the trees.
Looping rainbows rolling by,
Quick as dewdrops,
Leaving cloud-filled skies.

Adore this day of January. March will be here in a hurry.

A Spring Day

One spring day not like another
Brings the wrath of season's clutter.
Celebrate these rare, unusual days,
A time of real change just for you,
Changes that are unusually powerful
And spiritually gratifying too.

A flicker of sunshine before the rain
Trickles down your shoe.
These sudden changes
Quickly burn images into your mind.

Uprooted trees, overflowing streams,
Unmanageable pools of water too,
Seemingly take away the fear
Of earthquakes, tornados, and lightning beams.

Gradual changes are welcomed,
No matter what it seems,
But limitless blooms of plants and flowers
Drop the leaves to earth for hours.

That short journey back to winter's wrath
Is not just a fling begot of fall.
Perhaps it's a blissful season's squall.
It is spring. That's all! That's all!

Falling Brown

Golden leaves fall to the ground,
Turning and brown.
Swirling winds blow debris,
Circling from the nearby trees.

Say hello to January.
Start the year anew.
February came much too fast.
2002 was hard to grasp.

Look at March and April's spring.
Now go on to May and June—
Party tables, food, and fables,
Cookouts way past noon.

July has its sweltering heat.
Dried-up August would not weep.
Summer drought seems all about
All the leaves turn green to gold.
September's treasures, October's woes.
On the ground, the leaves are brown,
Crumbling under autumn's now
Inhibitions and winter's wrath.
Nature's reason is food for grass.
Each new season soon shall pass.
Live each day from first to last.

In the Great Room

Sunrise! Sunrise! That bright spring morning.
Warmth gently kisses stained glass windows.
Clear light begins to bounce off awnings
Upon artistically crafted windowpanes.
Seamless, colorful rainbows
Touch the swirled marble flooring,
Woven just below tightly chiseled tapestry,
Every color-enhanced hue brightly glowing,
Shades of red, blue, yellow, and orange.
Green and purple appear,
Truly kissed by the sun.

With each hue inseparable by human eye,
Breathtaking mirrored views
Extract both moan and sigh.
That warmth is an open invitation from the sky.
A beautifully multicolored crystal vase
Reflects warmth all over this place,
Shining much like heavenly stars,
Arching rainbows from here to Mars.
But in an instant,
Shadows gracefully fall across this sunlit room,

Snuffing out light,
Where once there was beautiful bright.
Then comes the gloom!
Gone are the rainbows,
The colors, that warmth of nature
That natural sunlight from less bright skies.
Gone! Gone! Gone!
In the twinkling of eyes.

CHAPTER TWO

Dedication

The Dentist

I sit and sit, but no one comes.
It seems time has passed me by.
Where is that dentist?
I just keep waiting for him. But why?
More patients arrive and pack the floor.
He has forgotten me for sure.
Holding my temper as best I can,
I wait my turn. Again! Again!
I manage a chuckle, but tempers are bad.

Some folks are belligerent and steaming mad.
I check my watch.
Two hours have passed.
Since coming here, not first not last,
I hold out hope my name they'll call
And peel me off this miserable wall.
I check my watch once more for time.
But clocks have stopped at half past nine.
I check his schedule just once more.
I can find no match with his for sure.
The dentist is on duty, you see.
But not today, no not for me.

Fly

You can fly without fear.
Miracles can really happen anywhere.
Was it your idea, or was it mine?
Or was it ours all of the time?
Happiness, sadness, pain, gladness,
Wonders do happen and overcome madness.
You're in or out. You're up or down.
Here, there, and everywhere.
Always and ever smart and clever,
Off and on, though brutally scorned.

Do what you want or what you will.
Whatever you do, just don't stand still.
Then you can fly way up to the sky,
Not just with wings, but with other great things.
Fly! Fly! Just like a bird up in that sky
Or like that baseball soaring by.
Fly! Fly! You can fly.
Open your mind, and open your heart.
Give yourself a healthy start.
Fly as though you do have wings.
Use your head to do great things.

Think of places you've never been.

Eagerly go there. Yes, you can!

Be free without as well as within.

Yes, you can fly again and again.

Fly not for me, but fly for you.

Your wildest dreams can now come true.

You can FLY!

You can FLY!

You can FLY!

Play Ball

Wake up, team!
Stretch! Stretch! Stretch!
Flex your limbs from head to toe,
Arm to arm, to and fro.
Run, throw, hit, and catch.
No ball playing, not just yet.
Everyone must pass this test.
Watch that sweat fall from your chest.
Favor goes to all the best.
Distinguish yourself from all the rest.

Warm-up rituals began.
Try to do the best you can.
Practice practice all you know.
Heightened pressures, there they go,
Quieted only by the love of money,
Playing a boy's game, and lying without trying.
You must make it to the biggest show.
You hear the crack of bats and balls.
Home runs sailing over walls.
Nerves are frayed with panic so near.
Line up quickly. Game time is here.

Responsibility, dedication, preparation, skill,
Trying to win with all your will.
Hit that ball far as you can.
Keep on running. You're the man.

No Workplace

On April two, you were no fool.
You left that sinking workplace pool.
You worked all those years and gave your best
Through mergers, acquisitions, and all the rest.
You left your friends.
They love you dearly nonetheless.
You showed such care to hang in there.
Many of your projects went nowhere.
You worked in groups and on the phone,
Even times when left alone.

We all have trials and tribulations new,
Deserving words of kindness too.
You have worthiness to come out here
And breathe the freshly driven air.
So go on out there while you can.
You paid your dues to the fellow man.
Go out and start your life anew.
That day you picked was April two.

On the Job

A job may not be based on
Abilities, ideas, formal suggestions,
Or how well one gets along with others.
Positions are occasionally held
By a known incompetent
Who has jumped ahead
Of some other hardworking stiff,
Trying to make ends meet,
Thinking he has arrived
And made the grade.

Be careful!
Such confidence may be short-lived.
It's not the most impressive path
Involving that not-so clever trait,
The typical do or say anything person.
That no holes bared individual.
Who uses any method to succeed.
This is often your typical screw-up.
That will somehow make it any way.

One Man Built That House

One man built that house,
Where you have lived all this time,
Where you have loved, laughed, and cried,
Where you have stayed since infancy,
Long before you were a bride,
Where you reside with privileged pride.

One man built that house.
Not that much different from all the rest,
A firm foundation from the start.
Footers border every part of ground,
Built with the best materials found.

Quick-dry mortar was poured and measured,
Leveled straight and neat.
He toiled in sweat and that boiling heat.
Tons of wood and metal were honed to bend
With screws, nails, and bracket ends,
All bonded into woven links,
It was able to withstand the forces of tornado winds
Forging through with tons of pressure,
Thrust upon that sloping rooftop
With a force intended to move all obstacles.
No matter how precisely measured.

One man built that house.
He worked by day and morning light.
He worked weekends deep into night
With hammers, wrenches, measuring rings,
Tools of the trade, and a few other things.
He raced to beat the winter hail,
The rain, the sleet, and the snow.
Oh, that was so many years ago.

One man built that house.
You'd never know it.
Just check the bricks and mortar now.
It doesn't even show it.

Back in the Workplace

Attention, employees! Management is here!
There'll be no fraternizing and harmonizing,
No romanticizing, exercising, or ritualizing.
You're on the clock.
You're mine, and I will keep you in line.
All of your rights belong to me.
Management can do no wrong.
You see!
You're on the clock.

Do it my way, or take the highway.
Did I mention the new policy in play?
You should have asked about it the other day.
You just can't win.
So take your pay.
You might survive another day.
This will get right under your skin.
No matter! No matter! You just can't win.
You're on the clock.
There'll be no whining, dining, moaning, or groaning.
Surely there'll be no telephoning.
Don't read that newspaper.
You'd better not stare.

Don't cry the blues when I'm in here.

The clock is my friend, and your time is mine.

Just do your work, and you'll be fine.

Now go on home where you think you're king.

I got your mind.

That's everything.

You're on the clock.

CHAPTER THREE

Responsibility

Busy

Always in a hurry.
Won't stop for a glance.
Busy! Busy! Busy!
Me stop? Not a chance!

Images haunt you day or night.
Personal feelings of fear and fright.
Peaking interests in future plans.
Hopes and dreams become demands.
Busy! Busy! So it seems.
Convenient ends instead of means.

Take some time to smell the air.
Communications everywhere.
Marking time can save a day.
Complications all the way.
Busy! Busy! Seek and search
Wonders of life's peaks and perch.
Slow down and live; control the helm,
That which tends to overwhelm.
Collect or purge those treasured gifts.
Deeds are really choices made.
Just pick the ones that make the grade.
We make the time for what we must.
Then choose the things that interest us.

Milda's Day

She left the bus quick as can be,
Clutching the clothes she got for free.
Her dress is all torn and tattered,
Like so many of her belongings through the years.
Look at those shoes! Her stockings sag.
Her worldly belongings are all in one bag.
Often she doesn't know one day from the rest.
Oh, Milda! Oh, Milda! You gave it your best.
It was the luck of the draw, though unkind and cruel.
She gathered her strength and worked like a mule.

Her hair was unkept. Her face was pale with gloom.
Her hands were both wrinkled
From mop tops and brooms.
The park bench was waiting for her to arrive.
As soon as she got there, she slid on its side.
Perhaps she could sleep until morning comes.
She must quench this great hunger and bathe in the sun.
She will stay strong for tomorrow and must let this day end.
She gets back on that bus and starts over again.

The Coveted Lane

Driving way down the highway,
Traffic rolls through.
Long white lines become a blur
While keeping me from you.

From pinhole to pothole, and more in front of me,
We're jammed in traffic as far as eyes can see.
The faster you drive, the smaller the rows.
Let's go! Get there just before the snows.
We're comfortably nestled in safety zones,
Driving to shelters and fomforts of homes.

Reckless drivers flashing by,
Disappearing in the sky.
Lanes as tight as a parking lot.
Danger lurks where calm is not.
Every vehicle is in its place.
Not to pass is no disgrace.
A lane is such a coveted space.
Check the left and then the right.
Eighteen-wheelers roll in sight.
Reckless drivers acting like clowns.
Social media hangs down.

Tires bounce off bumps and slippery roads,
Spinning, spinning, spinning from heavy loads.
One car rolled over and stopped again.
It dared invade a coveted lane,
Jeopardizing safety and driving folks insane.

Valued lessons were learned that day,
Though not absent of great pain.
No snow to show.
No wind, no sleet, or no hail.
And not a drop of rain.

Change Lives

A change shall come into our lives—
To be nurtured,
To be taught,
To be loved,
To seek leaders to lead and not be led,
To study the examples readily set,
And restart those things that failed.

Many changes shall come
To you and me.
They shall teach us better ways
And then look to us for greater days.

There shall be love, respect, and maturity
Passed through knowledge and purity.
Changes shall come to open our minds,
Undaunted at all by Father Time,
Unaltered by the evolution of man.

They shall come in a natural sense.
And with that deep understanding
Of everything demanding,
With change, we shall thrive.
Change is alive.

CHAPTER FOUR

Truth

Life

Like the wind blowing through your hair,
Like a brisk run in the morning,
Like floating down a liquid stream
Before the day's adorning.

The breaths you take so effortlessly,
The sounds that are within,
That everlasting warmth you feel
That never leaves your skin.

This life you live and hold so dear
And stays within you through the years.
That well-known gift the one we get
And use as if we paid for it.

Cities Don't Sleep

Sirens blast through the night.
People moving under light,
Some folks are content, but others with fright.
In and out of cars, leaving restaurants and bars,
They smoke cigars while studying the heavenly stars.
Midnight comes too soon.
Then clocks strike one.
But morning seems to never come.
Marking time is not much fun.
Then comes daylight brightened by the sun.

Deafening noises pierce the ear without reason,
Regardless of the season.
We must bolt right out of here.
Some jobs start while others end.
You think you know what's coming.
Just when and where are these reflections?
Strangers come from all directions.
Some are with friends humming their tunes.
Morning hassles end way before noon.
But night will come too soon.

Girl Child

Born the year 1999 on that twenty-first of May,
A warm and wonderfully clear spring day.
Surely a gift from God—that precious new member to family and friends,
Quite special to those of very next kin.

Yet a Gemini for sure.
What a blessing and much more—
A welcomed addition to this family.
Then there was the Gemini three.

Her beauty rivaled her smarts and more
And echoed through her very core.
So pleasant to be around, all so loving and caring,
A rare jeweled crown yet not overbearing.
No wiser a child can be; she reads like a champ and writes like pros;
Lights up each room wherever she goes.
Not really a surprise on any day.
Able to do most things her way.
No doubt she will succeed in all of life's pursuits.
Ability to spare and charming to boot.

Lost Keys

We can go nowhere. The keys are there.
Somewhere! Somewhere!
Daylight has come. Night rest is done.
The morning comes too soon.
Where is that fourth-phased moon
To light my way?
After crickets start to swoon,
Two locks rest in felt-lined trays.
I need those keys to start the days.
Keys are lost for now and later too.
They may be near. Sure wish I knew.

Medicare Man

Medicare man, there you stand.
You hold that powerful card in hand.
Now cash in on that well-earned check
Sent by wireless Internet.
You worked a lifetime in the nighttime
Until the morning's blue.
You can't believe your dream came true.
It took a long time getting here.
You reached the place that's held so dear.
You made it to that phantom ship.
Then you came aboard and never slipped.

You worked so terribly hard
To earn a meager pay.
Benefits have finally come your way.
You're so glad to be sitting there,
Actually getting health and care.
Medicare man, who is he?
Could be you! Could be me!

Birthdays

A day unlike any other,
Its own character, identity, and purpose
That annual time of year,
All so revealing,
That less than gradual change
With fears not so willing.

Seasonal surroundings remind you it is near,
That one event anticipating,
A celebration unique
Only to your being.

Yet a perfect time for
Reflection, recollection, and introspection,
A time to make that special effort
To hear, see, feel, and smell,
To taste life's treasure,
That substance of which dreams are made,
Your annual event.

Boy Child

Born early that Monday morn in 1995,
A balmy January day,
He arrived with unmistakable vigor and pride.
Dad laid him gently at his mother's side.
He smiled, kicked, and even cried.
This young man can't be confused or wronged.
He'll challenge you until your tongue hangs long.
A better player you're not likely to see.
Computer games are all in his mind.

There's track and field and a few other kind.
His skills are good in school as well as out,
Some not so great to speak about.
He reads, writes, and understands
Some things not known to every man.
He stands his ground as matter of course,
He's as stubborn as they come.
He's such great fun to be around,
Even when he acts the clown.
At his young age, he's not a bore.
Much wiser than his years for sure.
You'd think he's been here long before.

Choices

Life is built on the choices made,
Not void of those discarded.
Mark the time, and some will fade.
They are considered not to make the grade
While others have departed.
Choose all the things you love the best.
But make some time for all the rest.

CHAPTER FIVE

Faith

Time

Walk along the moonlit trails.
Step slowly with tender cares.
From nowhere comes the rising sun.
Feel its warmth though you are done.
Step up the pace to close the gap.
Must win this race; time is the trap.
Time has gone by from moon to sun.
That time the time to have some fun.
The trap has sprung, but I am free.
And pleasantness abides with me.

Saints

Young, middle-age, and senior saints
Offering their services no matter how quaint
All for the betterment of man,
Your God is right there by your side,
Everywhere you reside.

Work, work, work, then take your rest.
Hold His yoke upon your chest.
For the sake of man, His presence is best,
Intoxicating righteousness
For goodness sake, divine holiness,

Strength born of weakness,
Humbleness, and meekness.
Learn of Him to learn Him.
Know of Him to know Him.
Believe in Him and show Him.
Never to outgrow Him.

Cherished Times

Spring days blend to summertime,
Not like all the others.
That time of year of gradual change,
From warm to hot where seldom is rain,
Celebrate!
These are nature's progressions
Through the seasons.
The time has passed and could not last.
Soak in each day in every way.
See, hear, feel, smell, and taste the beauty.

Nature's gifts leave too soon,
And through it all, we move so fast.
Then see what life is all about
And what it really means at last,
Those things that fill
Those wonders of every dream,
Future, present, and the past.

Better than Yesterday

That ancient wall phone
Just rang and rang like I'm not here.
It made me jump up from my chair.
I must block that call tying up my line,
Ringing now the twentieth time.
High up on the wall for sure,
Please don't let it ring no more.
Silent at night, the quietest of storms,
I prefer it that way.
Where's that busy signal when you need one?

If they're pushing sales on me,
I got my script for them to see.
I'll make them squirm
And drop some tears.
Do dial my number if you dare.
No more high-pressured hype in my ear.
I can't be a prisoner in my own home.
Just let it ring, but leave me alone.

Friends Are Friends (or Not)

Friends stick together ...
Like artful colors of a master painting,
Like the fingers in a soft leather glove,
Like glue bonding the heels of a thousand shoes waiting to be worn,
Like the voices of Pearl Bailey, Whitney Houston, Diana Ross, and Ray Charles all blended as one,
Like the warmth of a summer's sun feeding each new blade of grass.

Friends are friends ...
Like nourishment is to the body,
Like spirit is to the soul,
Like stars lighting the way from a moonlit midnight glow,
Like all humanity living under man's rules but playing to their very own tune,
Like Miles Davis, Louie Armstrong, Wynton Marsalis, and John Coltrane each expressing the same note
In their own harmonic way but wrapped around one melody.

Friends are friends. *Or not!*

The Clocks

Set the clocks.
It's time to spring forward.
Reset the clocks; set them back
To where they were last fall
When you thought
You had saved an hour of time
Before that wake-up call.
Set the clocks back.

It's time to spring forward
Toward what you thought.
Was some magic hour saved
When you thought you were moving time,
Grabbing an extra sixty-minute hour,
Three thousand and six hundred seconds?

You can't capture time.
Nor move it back and forth.
You've simply moved your schedules
To another place.

It's all a delusional pretense,
An extremely poor substitute for truth,
A thinly disguised exercise in futility.
Reality sets in when you finally realize.
You evolve around time,
Not time around you.

Changing Times

Non-traditionalism
Is as exciting as scooting to the front
Of a 1970s gas line,
As rare as an honest politician.
The former can be dangerous and expensive,
Depending on what you're driving.
The latter may simply be impossible.
We no longer gauge miles per gallon,
Nor miles per hour.
Rather, we peek at our gauges to determine
How many gallons of gas we use per mile.

Truth-telling and politics
Should not be used in the same sentence.
Ask any unsuspecting citizen.
Look closely enough!
You may see one
Waiting for some positive change,
A direction that seldom appears,
But may stun you on occasion.

CHAPTER SIX

Emotion

Sweet Words

Think them; read them.
Write them, and hold them.
Study them; show them.
Try to get to know them.

Sweet words of bliss and coy,
Sweet words of hope, sweet words of joy,
Sweet words of faith and accomplishment,
Success and failure too,
Sweet words of the world,
Sweet words of life's struggles and strife—
You know they're sweet each time you meet.

The words you find so easy to say,
No matter how fast they come your way,
While gained through fear or confidence,
By experience, independence, or dependence,
By study, accident, or force,
They're usually spoken as matter of course.
Sweet words!
Sweet words!

Dream Baby

When baby awakened from his sleep,
Mom was there to rub his feet.
He raised his head to leave the bed.
But Mom was there to hold instead.
Mom cuddled baby to stop his fall.
She smiled, and baby's frown was gone.
Her words fell gently on his ear.
Mom kissed sweet baby.
Sleep now, my dear.

More tired today than ever before,
She winked at baby and smiled some more.
No more to weep nor cry a peep.
Go back to bed and back to sleep.
Sweet dreams ahead at Mother's feet.

Wake-Up Dream

Soothing music to my ear,
Not so aware that it's so near.
Pops and crackles, note by note.
Strangest music ever wrote—
Noise and music, what a blend.
Woke me from this sleep I'm in.

I don't know just where I should begin.
The sounds are now so soft and soothing.
Rhythmic melodies sure are confusing.

Snap your fingers, and tap your feet.
Every note is now complete.
Wake up from this sudden trance.
Strike a natural-looking stance.
Folks stopped and stared; some headed home.
Some even used the telephone.
This quiet place of charm and bliss
Is now overwhelmed with busyness.
Pause for the moment's silence
While time has passed you by.

Standing in a single spot,
You dare not move with eyes wide shut.
Wake up! But not so sure you can?
The sounds of folks you clearly hear
Just drowning out the notes.
T'was just a dream.
But oh so real!

I Saw You

I saw you last night as you passed by.
Was that you gliding through the sky?
You wore that dark blue dress again.
I picked that out when we were kin.
Did you see me? Did you not care?
I know I saw you standing there
Out in that robust midnight air.
I did say hello.
Don't you know? Don't you know?

I saw you last night—not once but twice.
I saw you out there on the streets.
That chance encounter, what a treat!
My kindly thoughts would not suffice.
Peace dropped into my heart that night,
Freely thinking of old times.
Tick-tock! Tick-tock!
I never came that way before.
Gliding along singing our song
Is when I knew
We both were wrong.

Back to basics, tough as it may seem,
I saw you last night.
Oh, what a dream.
Or was it just a puff of steam?

Fair Maiden

Can closer friends we be?
Oh no! Not you and me.
Why not commit to what we've got?
To part no more would mean a lot.
Then closer friends this we will be.
No more misunderstood but free!
Do stay! And you will soon agree.
It's real.
Not just my fantasy.

Self-Esteem

Nobody can ever do anything to you
That you don't want him to do.
Nobody will ever do anything to you
That does not reflect how he feels
About himself or you.
You will never do anything to any human
That does not reflect how you feel about him
Or yourself.
If you did nothing this day toward your goal(s),
Then nothing happened. It's just wasted time.
Tomorrow will surely come.

Miss You

I miss you when you are away.
You were leaving yesterday.
Surely I'll miss you when you're gone.
Please come back some early morn,
Stuffed, puffed, sassy, and free,
Mad, sad, and glad as can be.

I see you each day, you're on my mind,
Not just now but all of the time,
Though you are there, I think I'm fine,
But alone and lonely without you,
Always thinking about you.

I'm missing you oh so very much.
Are you really near, or are you far?
I miss your aroma, your laugh,
Your winning ways,
The special sounds you make,
Your ferocious appetite for life,
Your unforgettable smile,
Those eyes that sparkle all the while.
And then there is your gentle stare
That always lets me know you care.

Trials of Life

Bandit, crook, pickpocket, and thief,
When will you slow and start to grow?
I heard what happened in Sin City last night.
After sundown, your game took flight.
A few local gun-toting, handcuffing,
Sunglass-wearing, donut-eating,
potbellied men in blue
Walked right up and started whipping on you.
There's no more hiding out.
Then you walked about like you did no wrong.

You forced illegal chemicals
Through every accessible vein in your body.
You sniffed white powder through your nose bend,
Like twin tunnels on toll roads that never end.
You sold those dangerous poisons
On every local street corner you see.
You risked the lives of others
For an instance of feel good.
There's no more time for smoke-filled rooms,
Counting cards and loaded dice all night,
Betting on everything in sight.

You're willing to gamble until morning light.
You took a mighty whipping that night.
You were forced to face the trials of life,
Those trials of life that test the very fiber of your being.

When seen, felt, bought then experienced.

Some are snorted or injected

But are never affected by you as you are by them.

Trials can turn life upside down

And are most times unsuspected.

But evil and greed can be challenged

Dismantled, displaced, crushed,

And even disconnected

Through emotions of one beautiful mind.

CHAPTER SEVEN

His Stories

The Twenty-First Century

Voting irregularities and controversies,
Vote counts, miscounts, and recounts,
Under-counts, over-counts,
And computer malfunctions.
The forty-third president takes office,
Courtesy of an Electoral College decision
Backed by the United States Supreme Court.
Pull the covers off, and shine some light on it.

School place violence is perpetrated
On students and by students
in cities as well as suburban America.
Shootings, killings, fights, and disturbances
Are all over the nation.
Then there was the so-called war on drugs,
A colossal misdirected use of resources
That focused only on the little guy,
Inner-city dealers hooked on designer drugs.
Follow the money trail.
Attack with vengeful legal forces.
Pull the covers off, and shine some light on it.

Sadly, jailed minority youths
Outnumber those attending college.
They are targeted, carted off to court, and then jailed

While many others
Go home to Mommy.
And Daddy never knew.
Pull the covers off, and shine some light on that.

CEOs, CFOs, COOs, CPAs,
And other corporate officials all hang in there,
Just long enough to suck out all the treasures.
Privileged groups benefit as matter of course
From unscrupulous insider trading,
That dubious gain woven from corruption.
And a vicious Wall Street turns its back on it.
Perpetrators retreat.

Well, before the bloodletting begins,
They sold those ill-gotten gains
Just before the roof caves in.
Look out, John and Jane Doe.
Shake, Mr. and Mrs. Average Citizen.
Wake up, Mr. Joe Six Pack and John Q. Public.
Gone are your nest eggs and your dreams.
Stock values drop like lead balloons
While others raise right hands,
Swearing no wrong was done.
Pull these covers off, and truth is revealed.

All Bets Are Off

I used to chauffeur you around
When you were so down and out.
I recall those daily loans you took.
Greenback singles, fives, and tens.
And there were twenties too.
It was my monies,
Hard-earned cash from my stash.

I forget how long it has been.
Back then, on me you did depend.
I now depend on you.

For every buck I gave,
You promised to give me two.
All bets are off.
I trusted you with credit cards,
My home, my life, my ride.
Never did I ever think
You'd tuck your tail and hide.

Now it appears I took your place.
Our roles are now somehow reversed.
Now I'm the one to fall in need.
I wish I could count on you,
As you once did on me.
Never in my wildest dreams,
Did I think you would turn and flee.
Not from me.

The Fighter

Strangers stare at his vehicle license plate in an attempt to assign a meaning to the personal display. The letters "RND ONE" are generally mistaken for the phrase "Round One." He's not a boxer, but he is occasionally mistaken for one, even though his demeanor is quite the opposite of the average ring dweller.

Do not let his soft-spoken, easygoing, quiet demeanor mislead you. Most of all, do not confuse his extreme kindness for weakness. While not a boxer, he is a natural fighter. At his side stands the greatest fantasized cut-man alive, patiently waiting and ready to administer first aid to quickly repair the slightest cut or laceration. However, the cut-man has never been summoned to action.

In his corner, you can see that well-known low-rise stool, a water bottle, and bucket, available for personal rejuvenation between rounds. Since nobody has ever laid a glove on him, he has never needed any of these tools of the trade. For these reasons, most spectators love him. Some dislike him because he ends every encounter long before they have time to warm their seats. He can go the distance, but nearly every encounter generally ends at round one.

He has scored thirty-two knockouts in thirty-three fights. Not one opponent went more than three rounds with him. If you believe that, I have another one to tell you.

After all, he's not a boxer, but he's quite the fighter.

What a winner!

Thoughts from Yesterday

Daunan was pleased as he arrived in Selma, Alabama, on that bright summer day. He then realized he had arrived at the site where Dr. Martin Luther King Jr. launched that historic 1965 Selma to Montgomery Freedom March. That particular historic event occurred during a time when Daunan's own parents would not have felt safe traveling to this city. He realized this was as somber a moment as any he had ever experienced during his early adult years. His mind drifted to thoughts of the many hardships his people had endured, especially during the 1960s.

By this day, thirty years after the march, the nation had made considerable progress in human rights and race relations. Daunan felt deeply honored as he waited for his connecting flight. He would soon be continuing his journey to Nashville to perform with a local country music group in a popular local nightclub that evening. Daunan had never previously set foot in either Selma or Montgomery. He came through Selma because his initial flight had been diverted to avoid an unexpected summer rainstorm.

While boarding Delta Flight 731 to Nashville, Daunan's thoughts drifted again. He pondered being in a part of the country that was completely foreign to him. He was totally unfamiliar with these surroundings. Nevertheless, he felt an unexplainable affinity though not having visited here before.

Daunan felt remorseful and actually regretted one thing. He simply should have been among those brave individuals who actively marched for the rights of their fellow citizens. He was well informed, and even at a young age, he believed he could have been directly involved in the struggle of the times. While many unfortunate circumstances personally victimized him as a young man, he remained a grateful recipient of incremental progress achieved for the masses.

On this day, Daunan thought back to the point in time when many of the opportunities and experiences he now took for granted were not available to his elders. He now realized that they were all products of past and present circumstances. He thought of those persons whom he loved so dearly. He felt the agony they had endured while confronting systematic and deeply rooted hatred simply based on race.

Daunan remembered a very compelling premise he had learned many years ago. He recalled that widely held premise that says, "If a person is told something repetitively, whether true or false, that individual begins to believe the premise as truth."

It is believed the human mind and body can and will adjust to the most difficult circumstances thrust upon it. A gradual transition exists, but it is not readily noticeable in the realm of what we experience as real time. Think "evolution."

Pockets (Never Burn a Hole in Your Money)

Sweaters, shirts, shorts, and shoes ... elbow patches ... holed-out socks ... pant legs drooping to the ground ... belts double wrapped around his waist ... jackets often draped to his knees. Little Chancy thought he was a poverty-stricken, poor boy. Chancy grew up in a small town just outside of the metropolitan area of a well-known northwestern city. He was part of a traditional close-knit, working-class family. His household included his stay-at-home mom; a grateful, hardworking dad; and seven siblings.

Chancy was the fifth child among four elder brothers and three younger sisters. His birth name was Louis Nathan, but they affectionately referred to him as "Pockets." Thankfully, Chancy eagerly wore most of the garments that his brothers passed down or discarded.

At times, winter coats hung far below his knees. Pant pockets occasionally kissed the tops of sweat socks he wore in double pairs to help cover holes and fill the excess space of oversized shoes. Layers of clothing generally protected him from the forthcoming bitter winters that were occasionally accompanied by an unsuspected storm. Little Chancy wore each garment with content and pride during most of his juvenile life.

He and the family always ate well and enjoyed the warmth of shelter, safety, and unconditional family love. He owned more clothes than he could ever wear out. While he innocently thought of himself as impoverished, he actually was not. This family enjoyed sustained financial stability through the years.

Each sibling eagerly participated in sharing all usable items of value and showed unwavering loyalty via unselfish family support. The practice is now an integral part of family planning, a sensible system now deeply entrenched within their family tree.

My Best Friend

I had a talk with my best friend last night. I speak with my friend regularly, and I know I have been heard. I have always had faith in my friend because my friend is all knowing. He sees and hears everything I say and do and knows and goes everywhere I go. My friend is my constant comforting companion.

I always call on my friend when I am in need, and my friend always guides me. My friend has never let me down, set a wrong path, nor ever forsaken me. My friend is at my side during good and troubled times. I always know who I am as well as who's I am. I constantly draw strength from knowing that my friend is with me always.

Strength flourishes among an unending faith and ability to handle those gradually progressively difficult obstacles placed in my path. My friend refuses to leave my side. For with my friend, I cannot fail. I may stumble, or I may fall. With the endless guidance of my friend, I will overcome all obstacles placed in my way.

I frequently call on my friend, be it night or day. With the help of my friend, I do believe, "All things are possible."

The Winds Blew

Patio awnings were twisted and torn,
Shredded like streaming rags.
Tree branches freely flowed
In symphonic harmony,
Hopelessly entangled end to end—
Twisting, cracking, and even breaking.
And the winds blew.

Toys and personal belongings
Tumbled through the streets,
Marking their way while rolling down the beach,
As if some unknown force possessed them.
Then came the hail, the freezing rain,
A touch of sunshine too.
And the winds blew.

Reams of trash rolled round and round,
Caught in jetlike streams,
As did most everything.
Trash can tops and contents too,
Thrown through the air.
Then they gently settled upon earth's ground
That just refused to move.
And the winds blew.
The winds blew and blew.
The winds blew and blew and blew.
I'm talking to you.

Glossary

CEO: Chief executive officer

CFO: Chief financial officer

COO: Chief operations officer

CPA: Certified public accountant

Eighteen-wheeler: Oversized vehicle

Footers: Construction foundation support

Fourth-phased: A phase of the moon

Great Depression: The 1929-1939 decade following the stock market crash, accompanied by high unemployment, poverty, low profits, and deflation

Insider trading: Use of privileged information to gain financial advantage prior to public awareness of that information

My ride: Personal mode of transportation

Ring dweller: Professional or amateur boxer

Slo-mo: As in slow motion and caught in a trance

Stash: Savings or other compilation of funds

Tools of the trade: Items or skills needed for tasking

War on drugs: A social and monetary "war" to enforce specific laws against trafficking drugs

About the Author

Ray Dunton is a native of Baltimore, Maryland, where he attended public schools. He has one son and three grandchildren. He pursues varied interests such as creative writing, travel, and sports. He has earned several certificates recognizing successful study and experience in computerization, video, and television production. Over the years, he has written opinion editorials that local newspapers published. *I'm Talking to You* is his first professionally published book.

Ray is retired from a successful thirty-nine-year career with the US government. He also enjoyed employment in private industry before and after his government career and owned a successful local video production company during the late 1980s.

He has traveled all over the United States and other countries. However, he has decided to continue living in the Maryland, Virginia, Delaware, and District of Columbia region where he can travel to many nearby historical places by automobile.

Ray appeared in a CNN special and local television stations to help explain his participation in a 1990s nationwide blood pressure study. This study was designed to determine whether potassium helps lower blood pressure.

About the Book

With the onslaught of today's social networking systems and continued developmental advances in electronics, personal communication has slowly faded. There is less personal interaction, and communication is systematically eroding. Social networking systems have greatly influenced the way we communicate with each other. However, nature maintains a more gradual process of less noticeable change. Albert Einstein once said, "I fear the day that technology will surpass our human interaction. The world will have a generation of idiots." Hopefully, our population will soon stop being so caught up in electronics that they are rendered unaware of their immediate surroundings.

Two common thoughts are apparent in this book: communications and forces of nature. This book presents comprehensive expressions of nature, dedication, responsibility, truth, faith, emotion, and stories through poetry, essays, and events, both real and fiction. It is a descriptive way to encourage readers to reconnect with the face-to-face communication we once knew.